Conversation Starters
for

Fannie Flagg's

The All-Girl Filling Station's Last Reunion

By dailyBooks

FREE Download: Get the Hottest Books!
*Get Your Free Books with <u>**Any Purchase**</u> of* Conversation Starters!

Every purchase comes with a FREE download of the hottest titles!

Add spice to any conversation
Never run out of things to say
Spend time with those you love

Read it for FREE on any smartphone, tablet, Kindle, PC or Mac.
No purchase necessary - licensed for personal enjoyment only.

or Click Here.

Scan Your Phone

Please Note: This is an unofficial conversation starters guide. If you have not yet read the original work, please do so first.

**Copyright © 2015 by DailyBooks. All Rights Reserved.
First Published in the United States of America 2015**

We hope you enjoy this complementary guide from DailyBooks. We aim to provide quality, thought provoking material to assistinyour discovery and discussions on some of today's favorite books.

Disclaimer / Terms of Use: Product names, logos, brands, and other trademarks featured or referred to within this publication are the property of their respective trademark holders and are not affiliated with DailyBooks. The publisher and author make no representations or warranties with respect to the accuracy or completeness of these contents and disclaim all warranties such as warranties of fitness for a particular purpose. This guide is unofficial and unauthorized. It is not authorized, approved, licensed, or endorsed by the original book's author or publisher and any of their licensees or affiliates.

No part of this publication may be reproduced or retransmitted, electronic or mechanical, without the written permission of the publisher.

Tips for Using DailyBooks Conversation Starters:

EVERY GOOD BOOK CONTAINS A WORLD FAR DEEPER THAN the surface of its pages. The characters and their world come alive through the words on the pages, yet the characters and its world still live on. Questions herein are designed to bring us beneath the surface of the page and invite us into the world that lives on. These questions can be used to:

- Foster a deeper understanding of the book
- Promote an atmosphere of discussion for groups
- Assist in the study of the book, either individually or corporately
- Explore unseen realms of the book as never seen before

About Us:

THROUGH YEARS OF EXPERIENCE AND FIELD EXPERTISE, from newspaper featured book clubs to local library chapters, *DailyBooks* can bring your book discussion to life. Host your book party as we discuss some of today's most widely read books.

Table of Contents

Introducing *The All-Girl Filling Station's Last Reunion*
Introducing the Author

question 1
question 2
question 3
question 4
question 5
question 6
question 7
question 8
question 9
question 10
question 11
question12
question 13
question 14
question 15
question 16
question 17
question 18
question 19
question 20
question21
question22
question 23
question 24
question 25
question 26
question 27
question 28
question 29
question 30
question 31
question32

- question 33
- question 34
- question 35
- question 36
- question 37
- question 38
- question 39
- question 40
- question 41
- question 42
- question 43
- question 44
- question 45
- question 46
- question 47
- question 48
- question 49
- question 50

Introducing *The All-Girl Filling Station's Last Reunion*

THE ALL-GIRL FILLING STATION'S LAST REUNION, WRITTEN BY FANNIE Flagg, brings to light the unsung heroes of World War II (WASPS), American women who flew military planes during the Second World War. In the book, Flagg gives these independent, innovative, and empire-building women their due recognition. The women featured in the novel were ahead of their time in that they were in charge of their own lives and businesses without any help from men. The book revolves around the lives of Sookie and her mother, and Sookie's relationship with FritziWillinkaJurdabralinski. In the midst of the story about Sookie, readers learn about the one thousand women that worked for the U.S. military during World War II. Most readers will discover the accomplishments and sacrifices of the WASPS for the first time because of Fannie Flagg's research.

Just like most of Fannie Flagg's novels, this novelis set in her home state, Alabama. Although this novel takes place in Point Clear, Alabama, Sookie's journey takes her to Wisconsin and California. The novel is primarily set in the present day but briefly travels back to the 1940s.

At the beginning of the novel, Sookie is nearly sixty years old and has a husband named Earle; they have four children. One day Sookie opens an unregistered letter that tells her that Lenore Simmons Crackenberry III is not her birth mother. Thus begins her search for her real birth mother, and she eventually learns that her birth mother is FritziWillinkaJurdabralinski.

Lenore Simmons Crackenberry III, Sookie's mother, is a true Southern matriarch. She is considered by everyone around her to be the life of the party, but Sookie sees her mother as overbearing.

FritziJurdabralinski is of Polish-American descent and worked at her family's Philips 66 gas station in the 1930s and '40s. She also served as a part of the WASPS during World War II. The gas station was transformed into an all-girl filling station when Fritzi and her sisters were forced to run the gas station by themselves.

Fannie Flagg based most of the characters in the book on real people. Fritzi's character was inspired by a WASP named Nancy, and Lenore Simmons Crackenberry III was based on Fannie's grandmother. Many of the other characters were inspired in part by different people in Fannie's life. Sookie and her mother, Lenore Simmons Crackenberry, have also previously appeared in another Fannie Flagg book, *Welcome to the World, Baby Girl!*

Introducing the Author

FANNIE FLAGG WAS BORN PATRICIA NEAL BUT DECIDED EARLY IN HER career to use a stage name because, at that time, there was an Oscar-winning actress named Patricia Neal. Fannie was raised in Irondale, Alabama by her grandparents. She was very young when she began her acting career, joining the Birmingham Theater Troupe when she was just fourteen years old.

Fannie Flagg moved to New York in 1965. While doing stand-up comedy, she got her first big break when someone offered to buy her material. After that, she became known as an actress and comedian, on both Broadway and television. Fannie Flagg is known for her 1970s and '80s appearances on the game show, *Match Game*. Fannie has appeared on talk shows such as *Good Morning America*, *The Rosie O'Donnell Show*, and *The Johnny Cash Show*. She has also starred on the big screen in *Crazy in Alabama*, *Grease*, and *Stay Hungry*.

Fannie Flagg is not only a talented actress but has also written successful books, including *Fried Green Tomatoes at the Whistle Stop Café*, whichwas made into a film in 1991 and was nominated for two Academy Awards.

Fannie Flagg never thought she would be a successful writer because she was a terrible speller, which is why she took up acting. She later learned that she suffered from dyslexia. In the 1970s, she took a break from writing because of her disability, but eventually overcame her struggle and decided to become a writer. She now talks openly about her dyslexia and the struggles it has caused her.

Fannie was influenced by writers like William Kennedy and Alan Ayckbourn. Her favorite book is *Travels with Charley*, which she rereads before she begins new work of her own.

In 2012, Fannie Flagg received the Harper Lee Award for distinguished Alabama writers. She considers it her greatest award because it came from her home state. Harper Lee showed up and surprised Fannie by presenting her with the award.

Discussion Questions

question 1

Fannie Flagg tries to educate readers on the WASPS role in World War II. Had you previously heard of these women before? Name some things you learned about the role of women in the war.

question 2

In the book, Sookie learns that her mother is not who she thought she was. How do you think Sookie's personality would have been different had she been raised by her biological mother?

. . . .

question 3

Fannie Flagg says that her book, *Fried Green Tomatoes at the Whistle Stop Café* inspired *The All-Girl Filling Station's Last Reunion.* What similarities did you notice between the two books?

. . . .

question 4

Fritzi is forced to take over the family gas station as a result of family circumstances. How do you think men in the 1930s and '40s felt about this decision? How do you think other women in that time felt?

question 5

Sookie is almost sixty years old when she learns the news about her mother. How do you think her reaction would have been different if she were twenty when she learned the truth?

question 6

After learning the truth about her mother, Sookie begins to question her life and the decisions she has made. What decisions is she referring to?

question 7

Fannie Flagg researched the WASPS for this story. Do you think she portrayed the women in a positive light? Do you think Fannie Flagg did a good job giving the WASPS their due credit? Fannie Flagg wrote *The All-Girl Filling Station's Last Reunion* coming off the success of *Fried Green Tomatoes*. Do you think she lived up to her fan's expectations? In what ways was *The All-Girl's Filling Station* better or worse than *Fried Green Tomatoes?*

question 8

Fannie Flagg makes sure that her stories, including *The All-Girl's Filling Station,* all have happy endings. Do you think this makes her stories predictable? Do you think readers prefer a happy ending? Why or why not?

question 9

Fannie Flagg regards the WASPS as pioneers in the women's movement. What are some of the ways the WASPS trumped female stereotypes of their day?

question 10

Sookie finds Lenore to be very overbearing and often finds herself in her shadow. Some say environment affects one's personality more than his or her inborn traits. Do you think this is true in Sookie's case?

question 11

Lenore is called "Winged Victory" because of the way she walked into a room. How might this symbol tie into Sookie's biological mother, Fritzi? Do you think Fannie Flagg was intentional in using a nickname that could be fitting for either of Sookie's mothers?

question 12

Fannie often writes about strong independent women in her books and *The All-Girl Filling Station's Last Reunion* was no exception. Tell about some of these women and what it was that defined them as strong and independent.

question 13

The WASPS did not receive much recognition for many years. Why do you think the WASPS story was so unheard of until now?

question 14

Fannie Flagg believes that the names in the South, as silly as they may sound to other people, are more of affectionate nicknames. Do you agree with her? What are some of the Southern names she uses in this book? Do they remind you of anyone in your life?

question 15

Fritzi shatters many stereotypes of her time. Do you think women have overcome these stereotypes? Explain why or why not.

question 16

Some people consider the book to be a self-help book because it encourages the reader to discover his/her personality. Was the book "helpful" to you? What about the book would cause someone to question their identity?

question 17

Some readers have praised the way Fannie Flagg was able to depict actual situations about real life. Do you agree? Why or why not?

question 18

Kirkus Reviews says that the book is "just the right blend" of both historical facts and fiction. Do you agree with the review or do you think the balance of the book weighed too heavily toward fiction given the importance of getting the story of WASPS out into the public? Why or why not?

question 19

Many reviews noted the plot twists and turns in the story. Do you think this made the book too difficult to follow or do you think this added to the anticipation of the story? Tell about one plot twist that stood out to you most.

question 20

Many reader reviews talked about Fannie Flagg's trademark humor. What do you think it is about her humor that seems to impress her readers? Give an example from the book.

FREE Download: Get the Hottest Books!
Get Your Free Books with __Any Purchase__ of Conversation Starters!

Every purchase comes with a FREE download of the hottest titles!

Add spice to any conversation
Never run out of things to say
Spend time with those you love

Read it for FREE on any smartphone, tablet, Kindle, PC or Mac.
No purchase necessary - licensed for personal enjoyment only.

or Click Here.

Scan Your Phone

question 21

Many readers remark that Fannie Flagg's characters have a quality about them that is always present in her novels. What is it about Flagg's characters that is so recognizable? Is there a particular characteristic or personality that is present? Explain.

question 22

One of the most common praises written about Fannie Flagg is her ability to tell a story. Do you agree that she is a good storyteller? If so, what is it about her writing style that has made her a successful author?

question 23

There are very few negative reviews about *The All-Girl Filling Station's Last Reunion*; however, one of the criticisms the book has received is that the present-day portions of the book did not live up to the history portions. Where do you think the modern-day story may have fallen short?

question 24

A reviewer referred to Sookie as a "caricature of a Southern woman." What do you think the reviewer meant by this and do you agree?

question 25

Some of the historical events have been questioned. Do you think that it is necessary to be 100% accurate about historical events when writing a fiction novel based on those events? Why or why not?

question 26

Fannie got her start as an actress and was very successful. In what ways do you think her acting career affected her ability to write novels?

question 27

Fannie's career in writing took off when she went to a writer's conference in Santa Barbara where she wrote a short story saying she was a twelve-year-old. She did this because she was embarrassed to make such spelling mistakes as an adult. An editor that was interested in her writing called her about developing the novel. Do you think the editor would have been interested if she had known Flagg was actually an adult? Why or why not?

question 28

Fannie was born as Patricia Neal but opted to use a stage name because another actress had the same given name. Do you think this was a wise decision on her part? What are your thoughts on the name she chose, considering she writes mostly about Southern characters?

question 29

Fannie was born and raised in Alabama but moved to New York City to pursue her acting career. This is where Fannie was noticed for her skit-writing skills, which eventually led to her becoming a novelist. Do you think she would have eventually become just as successful if she had stayed in Alabama? Why or why not?

question 30

Fannie had a significant presence on television in the '70s and '80s. Do you think this presence played a role in her success as a writer?

question 31

After Sookie finds the letter that reveals Lenore is not her mother, she sets out to find her biological mother. She conducts her search in secret. Why do you think she kept it a secret? If you were to learn such news, would you try to find your birth mother at such a late age in life?

question 32

Sookie has an identity crisis when she learns that her mother is not who she thought she was. This discovery has a great effect on her. How would this kind of revelation affect you?

question 33

Fannie Flagg says she grew up in a home with independent women. How do you think her upbringing affected the female characters in this story? How do you think the characters would have been different if she had grown up in a typical 1930s home?

question 34

Sookie and her best friend, Marvaleen, have different ways of dealing with their problems. Would you be more like Marvaleen or Sookie? List some ways that you might cope with divorce or an identity crisis.

question 35

Heritage and culture are a very important part of the book. Do you find that this is the case in your own life? What are some of the things you identify with in your culture that make you who you are today?

question 36

This novel is set in Alabama. How do you think Sookie and Lenore's characters would have been different if it were set in the Northeastern United States?

question 37

How do you think this story would have been different if it was written from Lenore's point of view?

question 38

Fannie Flagg struggled with writing because of her dyslexia, but she refused to give up. If you had dyslexia, would you have endured the struggle she did to become a writer?

Quiz Questions

question 39

FritziJurdabralinski was a _____ in World War II.

question 40

True or False: WASP stands for World Airline Services Pilot.

question 41

True or False: Sookie Poole is almost sixty years old at the start of the book.

question 42

Lenore Simmons Crackenberry III is Sookie's _____.

question 43

True or False: Sookie questions her identity when she finds herself in the midst of a divorce.

question 44

Sookie learns a secret about her mother after she finds a _____.

question 45

Fritzi and her sisters took over a _____ after her father became ill.

question 46

True or False: Fannie Flagg's given name was Patricia Neal.

question 47

True or False: Fannie Flagg made regular appearances on *Jeopardy*.

question 48

Fannie Flagg's bestselling novel is _____.

question 49

Fannie Flagg worked on the popular hidden camera show called _____.

question 50

Fannie suffers from _____, which has been a lifelong challenge for her writing.

Quiz Answers

1. pilot/WASP
2. False; Women's Air Force Service Pilots
3. True
4. mother
5. False; She learns a secret about her mother
6. letter
7. gas station
8. True
9. False; *Match Game*
10. *Fried Green Tomatoes at the Whistle Stop Café*
11. *Candid Camera*
12. Dyslexia

THE END

Want to promote your book group? Register here.

PLEASE LEAVE US A FEEDBACK.

THANK YOU!

FREE Download: Get the Hottest Books!
*Get Your Free Books with **Any Purchase** of* Conversation Starters!

Every purchase comes with a FREE download of the hottest titles!

Add spice to any conversation
Never run out of things to say
Spend time with those you love

Read it for FREE on any smartphone, tablet, Kindle, PC or Mac.
No purchase necessary - licensed for personal enjoyment only.

Get it Now

or Click Here.

Scan Your Phone

Made in the USA
Middletown, DE
19 October 2025